Words for all Occasions

ISBN: 1 84013 869 6

This edition for
Grange Books
Units 1-6 Kingsnorth Ind. Est., Hoo, Nr Rochester,
Kent ME3 9ND,
United Kingdom,
www.grangebooks.co.uk

Printed in Malaysia

Words for all Occasions

Michelle O'Regan
Erin Mew

Contents

Introduction

Have you ever been stumped by what to write on greeting cards for birthdays, anniversaries, thank you, bon voyage, missing you, condolences and the many other human occasions?

You've spent ages browsing the entire supply of 'big-brand' cards, and you haven't been able to find the message that is just right?

This book covers most of life's 'occasions' —the celebrations, the commiserations and the consolations.

Writing Notes and Cards

When we write a personal note or card we are telling the recipient they are in our thoughts.

Below are special points to keep in mind.

1. Don't write when you do not have the time to stop and think about what you wish to express.
2. Always use the recipients name, or if they are well known to you the use of their nickname may be appropriate.
3. If possible, try to connect the note with something important happening in their lives, such as the birth of a new baby, new job or engagement. Or focus on their hobby or even their weaknesses, in a light and humourous way.
4. If you are sending a gift with the card, explain why you bought that particular item for them.
5. Sometimes using an appropriate quote helps start a note.
6. Use real and natural conversation in your note. Try to avoid sounding dull, stiff or impersonal. However, do not use real conversation to the extent that it sounds tacky. Try and avoid using slang and colloquial language.
7. Closing a letter depends on how well you know the person. Many people use 'love' but in some cases this may be inappropriate. Some alternatives may be 'warmly', 'fondly' or 'affectionately'.

CELEBRATE THE DAYS

Writing Birthday Notes

Birthdays are very personal occasions and depending on the year being celebrated, it can be either 'just another' birthday or a significant milestone. When writing a birthday note, it is important to consider how the recipient may feel about this birthday and other things happening in their lives. If there has been a recent death in the family, for example, a funny or silly card may be inappropriate.

The best thing to do when writing a birthday note is to make sure the receiver feels special and unique!

Some different styles for birthday greetings may be:

1. Witty and clever
2. Gracious
3. Mention your friendship or relationship and how much it means to you.

When buying a birthday card, do not buy the first one you see, take time to select an appropriate card.

Birthdays

Birthdays—General

Once a year on just this day,
We cheer, we eat, we get to say
Hip hip hooray
Yes it's your birthday!

May your birthday be bright and beautiful and filled with joy.

May this year bring you close to all you wish to achieve.

Party and presents
Cake and candles
Birthday time again!
So happy that you're here
To give us all good cheer.

May your birthday be filled with love and laughter.

Another birthday
Oh what fun
I get to have my way
And wish you a very special day
And sing Hip, Hip Hooray!

To a dear friend who has always been there. Happy Birthday.

We can light the candles on your cake now, the fire department has been alerted!

It's YOUday TOOday
Let's celebrate!!

Born naked and screaming
Cause to celebrate!
You might get lucky again
Happy birthday!

Birthday wishes to you on your special day.

Like fine wine and mature cheese
You're not getting older
Only better.
Happy birthday!
May all your wishes come true!

You're the icing on the cake.
The twinkle of the candle's flame
The reflection of all those smiles
We shared.

Many Happy Returns!

Every birthday holds the promise of a new beginning.
I hope this is the start of a wonderful year for you.

I hope you have a wonderful birthday.

When you're a kid
Birthdays seem to take forever
To come around
When you're older your head spins
From the speed at which they fly at you.

Happy birthday little child
Your face all bright and shiny
Your whole body wriggles with delight
At all the presents and the goodies
Have fun and we'll all enjoy YOU
It's your big day
So party on and make each moment special
Happy birthday!

When things start to drag and things start to sag, when you think about it, they don't look too bad!

We gather together
Each year to celebrate
How much we love you
And how glad we are,
that your mother had you!

How fast the years have flown
How tall and strong you've grown
Have fun with your friends
And a very happy birthday!

Wishing you happiness on your birthday, forever and always.

May your birthday, like you, be special.

To a special person
On (*her/his*) birthday
May your day be filled with happiness
Amongst your friends and family who love you.

Son
Now you're (*state age*) my darling son
How tall and strong you've grown
I hope this day is so much fun
The best you've ever known

Daughter
Now you're (*state age*) my lovely one
How fine and fast you've grown
I hope this day is so much fun
The best you've ever known

Birthdays Special

First Birthday

Darling (*insert name*), You have brought us much joy over the past year and for that we thank you very much and look forward to sharing the rest of your life with you. Happy Birthday. Congratulations on reaching your first birthday.

May you have many more to come.

Happy First Birthday!
May your life be long and filled with joy and happiness.

May this be the first of many birthdays to come.

There was a star that danced, and under that were you born.

Eighteen

Congratulations! Remember, you are now legally responsible for your own actions!

May the next eighteen years be as fantastic as the first eighteen.

Congratulations on reaching the first of many milestones. Happy Birthday.

Welcome to a new phase in your life. May all your wishes and dreams for the future come true.

Twenty One

So you've already had the keys to the house and the car for a while now – but I'm hoping today will bring you the key to happiness and health.

Congratulations! What a splendid age – no one ever complained about reaching this milestone – enjoy every day of it!

Happy 21st Birthday! May this next phase of your life bring you everything you wish for.

May the next twenty one years of your life be as fulfiling and as exciting as the past twenty one years. Congratulations!

Forty

Life begins at 40 so we've all been told
And those older than 40 welcome you to the fold.

You're not 40, you're eighteen with 22 years experience.

The first forty years of life give us the text: the next thirty supply the commentary.

At twenty years of age, the will reigns; at thirty, the wit; and at forty, the judgement.

A man of forty today has nothing to worry him but falling hair, inability to fasten the top button, failing vision, shortness of breath, a tendency of the collar to shut off all breathing, trembling of the kidneys to whatever tune the orchestra is playing, and a general sense of giddiness when the matter of rent is brought up. Forty is Life's Golden Age!

Fifty

The beauty of aging is that the older you get the less it matters whether your hair is in place, you have a nice figure, your makeup is perfect—you've learned that happiness comes from the inside—and the petty things don't matter.

50 is a splendid age,
and deserves a special verse
but look at it another way
Half a century sounds much worse!

Forty is the old age of youth; fifty is the youth of old age.
- Victor Hugo

Getting Older

Remember, age is just a number! ...which keeps getting larger.

Age is an issue of matter over mind. If you don't mind, it doesn't matter!

Anyone who keeps the ability to see beauty never grows old.

A birthday is just the first day of another 365 day journey around the sun. Enjoy your trip!

You are only young once, but you can stay immature indefinitely.

Aged to perfection...

The good news is that the longer you live the longer you're likely to live.

Well-behaved women barely make history—so why don't you be happy, be mad, be free, be outrageous, wild and silly.

Birthdays are good for you—the more you have, the longer you live.

You used to look in the mirror in the mornings and find fault with yourself. Now you have the wisdom to have joy in the living of life! Happy birthday!

You're getting old when you get the same sensation from a rocking chair that you once got from a roller coaster.

Think on the bright side—you were brought up to respect your elders and now you don't have to respect anybody.

The consolation of growing older is that as you lose your mind, you don't miss it so much.

Belated Birthdays

Finding the perfect birthday card took a little longer than expected... Sorry I'm late. Happy Birthday!

I'm sorry I missed your special day. I hope it was a good one.

This comes a little late but this birthday wish is as good as new.

When things get busy, time slips by,
but birthdays never seem to wait
So when we finally send our thoughts,
they may be kind of late.

When it's someone special like you,
someone we like an awful lot,
Our thoughts are always right on time
It's just this card that's not!

From Afar and Across the Miles

Sorry I couldn't be there on your special day
And even though there are the miles between us
I carry you in my heart and will be with you when you celebrate.

Happy birthday—we may not be with you but you live in our hearts. Here's a wish that this year is a very special one for you.

Even if I cannot be there to share your special day with you, know that my thoughts are always with you.

The Consolations of Aging Quotes

And in the end, it's not the years in your life that count. It's the life in your years. –Abraham Lincoln

It is so comic to hear oneself called old, even at ninety I suppose! –Alice James

All would live long, but none would be old. –Benjamin Franklin

The first half of our lives is ruined by our parents, and the second half by our children. –Clarence Darrow

The hardest years in life are those between ten and seventy. – Helen Hayes

How pleasant is the day when we give up striving to be young —or slender. –William James

Zodiac Birthday Greetings

ARIES —The Ram

March 21 to April 20

Adventurous; energetic; pioneering; courageous; enthusiastic; confident; dynamic and quick-witted.

TAURUS —The Bull

April 21 to May 21

Patient; reliable; warmhearted; loving; persistent; determined; placid; secure and loving.

GEMINI —The Twins

May 22 to June 21

Adaptable; versatile; communicative; witty; intellectual; eloquent; youthful and lively.

CANCER — The Crab

June 22 to July 22

Emotional; loving; intuitive; imaginative; shrewd; cautious; protective and sympathetic.

LEO — The Lion

July 23 to August 22

Generous; warmhearted; creative; enthusiastic; broad-minded; expansive; faithful and loving.

VIRGO — The Virgin

August 23 to September 23

Modest; shy; meticulous; reliable; practical; diligent; intelligent and analytical.

LIBRA — The Scales
September 24 to October 23
Diplomatic; refined; romantic; charming; easygoing; sociable; idealistic and peaceable.

SCORPIO — The Scorpion
October 24 to November 22
Determined; forceful; emotional; intuitive; powerful; passionate; exciting and magnetic.

SAGITTARIUS — The Archer
November 23 to December 21
Optimistic; freedom-loving; jovial; good-humoured; honest; straightforward; intellectual and philosophical.

CAPRICORN — The Goat
December 22 to January 20
Practical; prudent; ambitious; disciplined; patient; careful; humourous and reserved.

AQUARIUS — The Water Carrier
January 21 to February 19
Friendly; humanitarian; honest; loyal; original; inventive; independent and intellectual.

PISCES — The Fish
February 20 to March 20
Imaginative; sensitive; compassionate; kind; selfless; unworldly; intuitive and sympathetic.

Chinese Zodiac

Born in 1924, 1936, 1948, 1960, 1972, 1984, 1996, 2008.
RAT: You are imaginative, charming, and truly generous to the person you love. However, you have a tendency to be quick-tempered and overly critical. You are also inclined to be somewhat of an opportunist.

Born in 1925, 1937, 1949, 1961, 1973, 1985, 1997, 2009.
BUFFALO: A born leader, you inspire confidence from all around you. You are conservative, methodical and good with your hands. Guard against being chauvinistic and always demanding your own way.

Born in 1926, 1938, 1950, 1962, 1974, 1986, 1998, 2010.
TIGER: You are sensitive, emotional, and capable of great love. However, you have a tendency to get carried away and be stubborn about what you think is right; often seen as a 'Hothead' or rebel.

Born in 1927, 1939, 1951, 1963, 1975, 1987, 1999, 2011.
RABBIT: You are the kind of person that people like to be around— affectionate, obliging, always pleasant. You have a tendency, though, to get too sentimental and seem superficial.

Born in 1916, 1928, 1940, 1952, 1964, 1976, 1988, 2000.
DRAGON: Full of vitality and enthusiasm, the Dragon is a popular individual even with the reputation of being foolhardy and a 'big mouth' at times. You are intelligent, gifted, and a perfectionist but these qualities make you unduly demanding on others.

Born in 1917, 1929, 1941, 1953, 1965, 1977, 1989, 2001.
SNAKE: Rich in wisdom and charm, you are romantic and deep thinking and your intuition guides you strongly. Avoid procrastination and your stingy attitude towards money. Keep your sense of humour about life.

Born in 1918, 1930, 1942, 1954, 1966, 1978, 1990, 2002, 2014.
HORSE: Your capacity for hard work is amazing. You are your own person—very independent. While intelligent and friendly, you have a strong streak of selfishness and sharp cunning and should guard against being egotistical.

Born in 1919, 1931, 1943, 1955, 1967, 1979, 1991, 2003, 2015.
GOAT: Except for the knack of always getting off on the wrong foot with people, the Goat can be charming company. You are elegant and artistic but the first to complain about things. Put aside your pessimism and worry and try to be less dependent on material comforts.

Born in 1920, 1932, 1944, 1956, 1968, 1980, 1992, 2004, 2016.
MONKEY: You are very intelligent and a very clever wit. Because of your extraordinary nature and magnetic personality, you are always well-liked. The Monkey, however, must guard against being an opportunist and distrustful of other people.

Born in 1921, 1933, 1945, 1957, 1969, 1981, 1993, 2005, 2017.
ROOSTER: The Rooster is a hard worker; shrewd and definite in decision making, often speaking his mind. Because of this, you tend to seem boastful to others. You are a dreamer, flashy dresser, and extravagant to an extreme.

Born in 1922, 1934, 1946, 1958, 1970, 1982, 1994, 2006, 2018. DOG: The Dog will never let you down. Born under this sign you are honest, and faithful to those you love. You are plagued by constant worry, a sharp tongue, and a tendency to be a fault finder however.

Born in 1923, 1935, 1947, 1959, 1971, 1983, 1995, 2007, 2019. PIG: You are a splendid companion, an intellectual with a very strong need to set difficult goals and carry them out. You are sincere, tolerant, and honest but by expecting the same from others, you are incredibly naive. Your quest for material goods could be your downfall.

Religious Occasions

Easter

Sunrise at Easter
Pearly pink and yellow glow
Radiating hope.

Sending you a basketful of wishes
For a very happy Easter!

Wishing you an Easter filled with love, peace and CHOCOLATE!

New beginnings, renewal of faith, miracles — may your Easter be full of blessings!

Hallelulia! Christ is risen
Let's rejoice — Happy Easter!

May Easter see the dawning of hope in your hearts and may you celebrate the joy of the season.

The Lord is risen
May you rejoice in the triumph of the risen Christ at Easter!

It's a blessed season that gives us the reason
To spread our love and good cheer
To light our candles in the church
And pray for all who're dear
Wishing you a Happy Easter!

Our Lord our Saviour has risen
To love us and protect us
And guide us on the path of life
Wishing you hope and peace at Easter!

God said, 'Let there be light
And there was light.'
Happy Easter to you and your family.

May each day bring with it
A new ray of hope to brighten your lives
And brighten your life with its guiding rays.

Love always protects, love always trusts, love always hopes — here's wishing you a Happy Easter!

Easter is a time of hope and joy.
So here's hoping you enjoy this Easter.

I love Easter! It gives me a great reason to tell you how much your friendship means to me.

Happy Easter. May your basket be filled with love and happiness.

Christmas and New Years Greetings from Many Countries Around the World

Argentine - Feliz Navidad Y Un Prospero Año Nuevo

Bosnian - Sretna nova godina

Brazilian - Feliz Natal e Prospero Ano Novo

Czech Republic - Vesele Vanoce

Cantonese - Gun Tso Sun Tan'Gung Haw Sun Sing Dan Fai Lok

Czech - Prejeme Vam Vesele Vanoce a šťastný nový rok

Danish - Glaedelig Jul og godt nyt år

Dutch - Vrolijk Kerstfeest en een Gelukkig Nieuwjaar /Prettig Kerstfeest

English - Merry Christmas and a Happy New Year

Esperanto - Felican Kristnaskon kaj Bonan Novjaron!

Estonian - Rõõmusaid jõulupühi ja head uut aastat!

Finnish - Hyvää joulua ja Onnellista uutta vuotta

Flemish - Zalig Kerstfeest en Gelukkig nieuw jaar

French - Joyeux Noël et heureuse année

Gaelic-Irish - Nollaig Shona Dhuit agus Bliain Nua Fe Mhaise

Gaelic-Scot - Nollaig Chridheil agus Bliadhna Mhath Ur

German - Frohe Weihnachten und ein glückliches neues Jahr /Frohe Festtage

Greek - Kala Christougena / Kala Khristougena kai Eftikhes to Neon Ethos

Hebrew - Mo'adim Lesimkha,

Hungarian - Kellemes karácsonyt és boldog új évet

Indonesian - Selamat Hari Natal dan Selamah Tahun Baru

Iraqi - Idah Saidan Wa Sanah Jadidah

Italian - Buon Natale e Felice Anno Nuovo

Japanese - Shinnen omedeto. Kurisumasu Omedeto. Akemashite Omedetô

Korean - Chuk Sung Tan / Sung Tan Chuk Ha.
Latvian - priecigus Ziemassvētkus un laimigu Jauno gadu
Lebanese - Milad Saeed wa Sanaa Mubarakah
Lithuanian - Linksmu sventu Kaledu ir Laimingu Nauju Metu.
Malaysian - Selamat tahun baru Die. Seihil as Slaynt Da'n Slane Loght Thie.
Norwegian - God Jul Og Godt Nytt Aar
Polish - Wesolych Swiat Bozego Narodzenia i szczesliwego Nowego Roku
Portuguese - Boas Festas e Feliz Ano Novo/Feliz Natal e um Prospero Ano Novo
Romanian - Sarbatori Fericite Sarbatori Fericite. La Multi Ani.
Russian - Vesyoloye Rozhdyestvo
Spanish - Feliz Navidad y prospero Año Nuevo.
Swedish - God Jul Och Gott Nytt År!
Tibetan - Tashi délek
Turkish - Noeliniz Ve Yeni Yiliniz Kutlu Olsun
Ukrainian - Srozhdestvom Kristovym / Veselykh Svyat i scaslivoho Novoho Roku.
Vietnamese - Chúc Giáng Sinh Vui Ve và Chúc Nam Mói Tot Lành
Welsh - Nadolig Llawen a blwyddyn newydd dda!
Yugoslavian - Cestitamo Bozic

Christmas

Christmas is a state of mind – it's up to us to dream and imagine it the way we'd like the season to be, and make it come to pass.

Christmas is like the magic wand waved over everything to make it warmer and more loving.

A season for giving
A season for love
Of goodwill and good cheer
Thank heavens above!

Little children love their Christmas
Can't wait to rise and shine
Giggles laughter happy sounds
Are soon to follow after!

The presents are signs of our love for each other.
Given with a smile, a hug and a kiss. Happy Christmas!

It's Christmas and we celebrate the birth of baby Jesus.
Thank You for sharing Your birthday with us.
So generous that we all get presents!

Around the world it travels. The spirit of Christmas. From home to home and heart to heart. How good to feel it spreading love!

Spread the love and caring
To more than just your own
Invite someone along to share in your day
After all its about sharing and finding room.

May your Christmas be a lovely one
With smiles and hugs and warmth
May the dinner fill you as well as the cheer.
And bring you again to the end of the year.

Yuletide is upon us! Ho hody ho ho!
Let's enjoy the time that we have with each other, the presents, the laughter, the good cheer and end again another year.

Merry Christmas and a Happy New Year. May the coming year be full of joy and happiness to you and your family.

We wish you a Merry Christmas and a happy and prosperous New Year.

May Santa fill your stocking with presents and may your home be filled with joy.

May God grant us everlasting peace.

Peace be to you and yours now and forever.

Passover

May your life be filled with the strength that can come with faith,
and the peace that can come with hope.

Wishing you a joyous holiday filled with light and love.

May the meaning of the season, being contentment,
joy and peace.
And throughout the days to follow,
may your blessings all increase!'

'We were slaves to Pharaoh in Egypt, but God took us out from there, with a mighty hand and outstretched arm...' Wishing you peace and blessings in abundance — on Passover, and always!

Passover is a season of promise... of hopes rekindled and love renewed, a time to reflect on what is truly closest to our hearts.

Passover is the perfect time to let you know that we are thinking of you. Bright wishes during this beautiful season.

Hanukkah

May the candle shine bright on Hanukkah.

May Hanukkah bring peace to you and your family.

Warm wishes for a happy Hanukkah

As we light the menorah at Hanukkah, thoughts of your love light up our home and our lives. Thank you both for all the labours of love, big and small, that have kept us close and helped me believe in myself. Happy Hanukkah.

Wishing you eight days and nights of happiness at Hanukkah!

Diwali

May the festival of light bring gifts to you and your family, richness in your lives, happiness to fill your home, and love in your hearts.

May success and joy light your way throughout Diwali.

May Diwali shower blessings upon you, and be the beginning of a year filled with happiness and riches.

Eid Al-Fitr

Warmest wishes to you and your family on this joyful and blessed day.

Wishing you a blessed Eid and happiness throughout the year.

May Eid bring us all closer together. Family and friends, united with faith and in joy on this happy and blessed day.

Cultural Occasions

Chinese New Year

Wishing you every success in the coming year.

May your New Year be filled with blessings and happiness.

Sending you warm wishes of happiness and prosperity for the new year.

Wishing you a year of success and happiness.
Have a wonderful year of the (____).

May this coming year be filled with all that you would wish for yourself.

To me every year seems like a new life.
Have a wonderful life in the new year.

May this new year be the best of your life.

Babies

Writing Births and Adoption Notices.

The basic reason for writing these notes is to celebrate a new member joining a family. Finding something unique about the baby such as first born, boy, girl, adopted, twins or born on a special day is a great way to start a note.

Remember to focus on the entire family, especially if this is not a first child. This is a special time for everyone in the family and this point should be acknowledged.

Unfortunately, some babies are born with illnesses, birth defects and other issues. In this case, the best idea is to keep the note short and sweet, as you may not be aware how the parents are dealing with the situation.

Birth of Baby

Ten tiny little fingers that always want to play,
That never stop exploring the wonder of today.
Ten tiny little fingers that from the very start,
Will reach out for tomorrow, yet always hold your heart.

Baby, baby softly sleeping how my heart goes out to you, how sweet your cheek, your tiny mouth, your tiny little fist!

Two tiny feet
That wave in the air,
Two little hands
That tug at your hair,

Whether it's a girl or whether a boy
Doesn't seem to matter
That baby is sure to melt your heart and bring you joy!

A baby is teddy bears, rattles and grins
Dining at midnight... giggles and pins!

You're the poem
I dreamt of writing
The painting
I longed to paint
You are the dreams
I had for my future
When I hoped for a life fulfiled
You are my child
And in all things I'm blessed!

Once I was a twinkle in my dear daddy's eye
My mother dreaming me up and gave a sigh
And ever since they've known that I was there you see
My mum and dad have waited to find out who is Me.

A new life! Is there any more wonderful signal of hope to any of us than sharing life with a child, who sees the world anew each and every day!

A lovely being as yet unmoulded, like a rose, its petals still folded.

When you are just a babe
No longer than a two hand span
You start to mirror their expression...
learn that smiling is the first sign of friendliness...
giggles and mirth and open gestures
win you many a smile and cuddle—
How lovely to catch on so quick!

Ah, it's a boy! How happy you must be to have been given this precious gift, a brother to (*sibling's name*). May he make you laugh more often than he makes you cry and surprise you with his antics and what comes out of his mouth!

A little girl! How wonderful to be able to watch her grow each day, beautiful and charming and totally disarming!

Little finger wrapped around yours, sleepy eyes opening onto a brand new world, skin so soft. Oh the charms of a new life, ah the promise of all the days to come!

A baby will make days shorter, bankrolls smaller, nights longer, love stronger, home happier, clothes shabbier, the past forgotten and the future worth living for.

How will your life change? Beautiful baby, happy house, silly smiles and goo-goos.

Baptism/Christening

May your baby's baptism be just the beginning of a life of faith that comes straight from the heart.

May this little scrap of life benefit from the grace of God. And grow strong and brave and honest

Bless you and the little life you have brought into the world. May your days be full of the little pleasures and joys of a child, and may he/she grow up to be a good Christian.

Welcome, precious little child
so fresh from God above.
Baptised today in Jesus' name,
held in His arms of love.

Lord, bless this tiny infant
who will make the world so fair.
Please keep this precious life
forever in Your care.

Congratulations and best wishes on your baby's christening.

How wonderful to celebrate your little one's special day! We were so happy to be there with you, and wish all good things in your future with this new life and the hope and joy it always brings to a family.

Let's wet the head of the new arrival, and welcome him/her into our lives! How lovely to be in on the very beginning!

We wish you a life filled with happiness, success and friendship.

Naming Day

Best wishes to your little one, whom we honour today in being witness as you give the child a name. A name to carry through his/her life — a name we will grow to love because it will bring to mind this unique person.

May your child's name be a blessing to all who hear it!

Arrival of Adopted Baby/Child

Congratulations and felicitations! We know how long you have waited for this day. We wish you all the joys that having a child in your life can bring you, and if you ever need a babysitter, we'd be very happy to oblige.

How wonderful for you to have this new life entrusted to you! We are so very pleased that it has come to pass and you have what you have so long wished for — may your days be filled with happiness.

You are a child of the universe,
no less than the trees and the stars;
you have a right to be here.
And whether or not it is clear to you,
no doubt the universe is unfolding as it should.
— Desiderata

How perfect! A new friend has arrived.
We are all blessed.

Little one, may your days be filled with sunshine and joy. May your nights be filled with the dreams you will live as you grow.

The miracle of a new life. A gift of hope and joy for the world.

Month	**Birthstone**	**Flower**
January	Garnet	Carnation
February	Amethyst	Violet
March	Bloodstone/Aquamarine	Jonquil
April	Diamond	Sweet Pea
May	Emerald	Lily of the Valley
June	Pearl/Alexandrite	Rose
July	Ruby	Larkspur
August	Onyx/Peridot	Gladiolus
September	Sapphire	Aster
October	Opal/Tourmaline	Marigold
November	Topaz	Chrysanthemum
December	Turquoise/Zircon	Narcissus

Rites of Passage

Rites of Passage

Writing for Rites of Passages — Bar Mitzvahs and First Communions/Confirmation.

These are major events in a young person's life. But being invited to celebrate an event, which is outside your own religion, may be daunting and cause for uncertainty. These notes are primarily for the children concerned and as a result it is best to keep the message short.

Bar Mitzvah

Congratulations on your Bar Mitzvah. May the knowledge you have gained bring you success and happiness always.

On Your Bar Mitzvah—Mazel Tov to You.

May the teachings of the Torah be your guide throughout your life.

Thinking of you with pride as you celebrate your Bar Mitzvah.

First Communion/Confirmation

We/I rejoice with you as you make this new beginning, praying the Holy Spirit will guide you always.

Best wishes on this special day. May it fill you with faith that will strengthen and inspire you always.

Warm wishes for you on this very special occasion.

Congratulations on your First Communion/Confirmation. Best wishes for today and throughout a future bright with promise.

Warmest wishes on this your special day.
May God watch over you all the days of your life.

God be with you.
Strengthen you
In sickness and in health
through all the days of your life.
May peace be with you always.

The angels rejoice and welcome you.

Weddings

Engagements

To the two of you
How happy we all are for you!
May your life together be full of joy and depth
We are here to support you and help you.

Two lives joined
How happy you've made your family and friends
You are both such wonderful people
And we are very happy you have found each other.

Congratulations on finding love together and on your decision to marry. Your engagement is something to celebrate and your marriage is sure to be beautiful.

Wishing you both a long life filled with great joy, much love, few tears and sweet times through all your years! Congratulations.

Warmest wishes on your engagement.

It is wonderful to hear that you are engaged. You both deserve so much happiness and I hope you can find it within each other.

Congratulations on your engagement.

Congratulations on taking that leap of faith. May your lives be long and happy together.

May you both live long and happy lives. Congratulations on this most happy occasion.

What force is more potent than love? May your life together be filled with sweet times and cherished memories.

Weddings

To the two of you — this is a very special day for all your family and friends and we are so happy to share in the celebration of your love and devotion — know that we are here whenever you need help and support.

When two people find each other and promise to spend their lives loving each other, giving support and encouragement and forgiveness over misunderstandings, this leaves all of us with a message of hope — best wishes for a rich and wonderful shared life.

May love always light your way...
May your marriage always be blessed.

A successful marriage requires falling in love many times, always with the same person.

May your marriage mark the beginning of a rich and wonderful shared life — no matter what life has in store it will be easier because you will be there for each other.

Two souls with but a single thought,
Two hearts that beat as one.

May you find your dearest friend, your deepest love, and your greatest joy in each other. Congratulations.

As you celebrate your wedding, know that others share in your joy and hope that all your married days will be as happy as this one.

Thank you for allowing me to share your most special day with you. Congratulations on your wedding day.

Congratulations on your marriage. May your lives together be filled with joy.

Today will be one of the most important and special in your life. Thank you for allowing me to be a part of it. Congratulations.

Wishing you a life filled with love, luck and happiness. Congratulations.

May the love you share always surround you, as you journey through life together as one.

May your marriage be the beginning of all you have ever longed for. Warmest wishes for a long and prosperous life together.

To love someone who loves you in return... this is the happiness everyone searches for.

May the honeymoon never end.

Acceptance and Rejection Notes

This is the most common form of acceptance and rejection note for wedding.

Handwritten acceptance
Mr. and Mrs. John Smith
accept with pleasure
the kind invitation of
Mr. and Mrs. Black
for
Saturday, 25th September
at 3:00 pm

Handwritten regrets
Mr. and Mrs. John Smith
regret that they are unable to accept
the very kind invitation of
Mr. and Mrs. Black
for
Saturday, 25th September

Handwritten split acceptance/regret
If more than one person has been invited, but not all are able to attend, the following form can be used:

Mr. John Smith
accepts with pleasure
the kind invitation of
Mr. and Mrs. Black
for
Saturday, 25th September
at 3:00 pm
Mrs. John Smith
regrets that she is unable to attend.

Handwritten acceptance with children
Mr. and Mrs. John Smith
Bianca, Adam and David
accept with pleasure
the kind invitation of
Mr. and Mrs. Black
for
Saturday, 25th September

Thank You Cards

Writing to a close friend or relative:
Dearest...,
It's beautiful and we love it! How thoughtful of you to give Andrew and I a treasured family heirloom. Grandmother's crystal vase will be my most prized possession. We thank you from the bottom of our hearts!
Love always,

Writing to a person you don't know very well:
Dear...,
Mother just gave me the silver salad servers you left and I couldn't wait to tell you how lovely they are. Andrew and I will think of you each time we use them. Thank you so very much.
Yours truly,

Writing to a Friend for a gift given as a group:
Dear...,
Thank you very much for the beautiful dinner set you so kindly gave us for our new home. Andrew and I now have a service for eight and are looking forward to using it for every special

occasion in our life. You are such a great group to work with and I appreciate each one of you.
Affectionately,

When writing a thank you note for a gift not really cared for:
Dear…,
Thank you so much for the cuckoo clock. We will think of you very time the little bird chimes. Looking forward to seeing you soon.
Sincerely,

When writing a thank you note for monetary gifts:
Appreciation for monetary gifts is expressed in the same way as a purchased item. If you have a particular item you intend to buy with the money, you can share that with them.

Dearest…,
Andrew and I want to thank you so much for the cheque you sent for our wedding. We have been saving for a deposit for our first home and have added your gift to our special account. It was so thoughtful of you. Someday soon, we will be inviting you to our housewarming!!!
Can't wait to see you and Uncle John again.

Your gift, so thoughtful, is a rare treasure.
Thank you.

My simple 'Thank You' seems so small compared to all you have given me.

Just when I needed you most, you were there.
Thank you.

Anniversary Gifts

Anniversary	Traditional	Modern
First	Paper	Clocks
Second	Cotton	China
Third	Leather	Crystal/glass
Fourth	Fruit/flowers	Appliances
Fifth	Wood	Silverware
Sixth	Iron	Wood
Seventh	Wool/copper	Desk Sets
Eighth	Bronze/pottery	Linens/lace
Ninth	Potter/willow	Leather
Tenth	Tin/aluminum	Diamond jewellry
Eleventh	Steel	Fashion/jewellry
Twelfth	Silk/linen	Pearls
Thirteenth	Lace	Textiles
Fourteenth	Ivory	Gold jewellry
Fifteenth	Crystal/glass	Watches
Twentieth	China	Platinum
Twenty-fifth	Silver	Sterling silver
Thirtieth	Pearl	Diamond
Thirty-fifth	Coral	Jade
Fortieth	Ruby	Coral/jade
Forty-fifth	Sapphire	Sapphire
Fiftieth	Gold	Gold
Fifty-fifth	Emerald	Emerald
Sixtieth	Diamond	Diamond

Thank You

Writing 'Thank You' Notes

Writing timely and thoughtful 'thank you' notes is an excellent way of expressing your appreciation to people who have provided you with assistance or kindness. You may not have liked the flowers or the food offered, but the most important thing is to thank people for their thoughts and good wishes.

There are certain events where thank you notes are appropriate and even expected and some, where it is simply a nice gesture. Weddings, Graduation, Bar Mitzvah, First Communion are a few that require it. Birthdays, Christmas and Anniversaries do not require a thank you note, unless the occasion was celebrated with a party and then a note is appropriate. It is usually best to send the note within two weeks of receiving the gift. Any later and you will appear unappreciative.

Six steps for writing a successful thank you note:

1. Greet the giver
2. Express gratitude
3. Talk about using the gift
4. Mention the past, allude to the future.
5. Thank them again
6. Give regards.

Firstly thank the person for the gift. Then mention the gift and how it will be used or has influenced your life. If you do not like the actual gift, you can focus on something else, such as the thought or the wrapping paper. The main thing to remember when writing a thank you card is to appreciate the time and trouble the person has gone to in giving you this gift.
Even if you have thanked the gift-bearer in person, it is still nice to follow up in writing. Make sure the note is sincere and meaningful. It does not need to be lengthy. Keep it sweet and short and filled with appreciation for the gift, hospitality or favour.

Each gift from each person needs to be acknowledged with its own thank you card. If a group of people all contribute to the same gift, it is appropriate to send a card to each person, thanking them for their contribution towards the gift.

'Thank You' in Many Languages

Afrikaans (Africa) - Dankie
Arabic - Sukran
Chinese (Mandarin) - Xie_Xie (shieh shieh)
Cook Islander - Kia Manuia
Croatia - Hvala
Czech – Dekuji (deh'-ku-yih)
Danish - tak (tahg)
Dutch - dank U wel (dahnk you well) (formal: thank you very much)
English - Thanks awfully, old boy
Estonia - Aitåh
Finnish - kiitos (kee'-toas)
French - merci (mehr-see')
German - Danke (dahn'-kuh)

Greek - Efharisto (ef-har-ris-tou')
Hebrew - Toda raba (thank you very much)
Indonesian - Terima kasih (teh-ri-mah kah-sih)
Irish - Go Raibh Maith Agat (Pronounced Go-Rev-Meela-Maw-Agut)
Italian - Grazie (grahts'-yeh)
Japanese - Arigato (ah-ree-gah'-toh)
Javanese - Matur nuwun
Latvian - Paldies
Lithuanian - Achu
Malaysian - Terima Kasih ('Tay ree ma Kaa seh')
Mali (Mandinka) - Abarka
Maori - Kia Manuia
Norwegian - Takk (tahkk)
Persian/Farsi - Mam'noon or Mo'teshake'ram (Spoken in Iran, Afghanistan and other Central Asian countries)
Philippines - Maraming Salamat (thank you very much)
Polish - Dziekuje (dsyehn-koo-yeh)
Portuguese - Muito Obrigado (Thank you very much)
Romanian - Va multumim frumos (great thanks)
Russian - Spasibo balshoye (big thanks)
Samoan - Fa'afetai tele lava (Thank you very much)
Scot's Gaelic (Many Thanks) - Moran Taing
Spanish - Muchas gracias (thank you very much, literally: many thanks)
Swahili - Ahsante Sana (Thank you very much)
Swedish - Tack så mycket
Tamil (India) - Nandri ('Nun-dry' spoken in South India, Singapore, Malaysia)
Tibetan - Thuk Ji Chhe
Wales/Cymru - Diloch yn fawr (thank you very much)
Zulu - Ngiyabonga

Friendship

Friendship

Old friends are scarce
New friends are few
Here's knowing I've found
The both in you.

You are one of the best things that's ever happened to me. You're my love and my best friend. And every day that goes by, it seems like I discover something new about you to love. It's incredible to me how one person can make such a big difference in my life. You touch my heart in a way I never knew before.

A friend who's true when you are blue
Who shares the laughs when e'er you do
Who holds the space when troubles come
And never counts the score or sum.

Finding a friend means
that we uncover a world
in ourselves
that would not have existed
if we had not found that friend.

Good friends are like stars... You don't always see them, but you know they are always there. Thank you for being my star.

Your true friend
Has the courage to tell you
Your lipstick is smudged
Your petticoat is showing…

It was by chance we met, by choice we became friends.

Your true friend loves you so well
That they risk your anger or upset
to tell you their truth.
Accept this gift of honesty.

To my dearest friend, thank you for always being by my side.

A real friend walks in when the rest of the world walks out. Thank you for walking in.

Remember we all stumble… it is a true friend who is there to catch you when you fall.

Promise you won't forget me,
because if I thought you would, I'd never leave.
—Winnie the Pooh

If I had one gift to give you, it would be the ability to see yourself as I see you, because only then would you know how extremely special you are.

Thinking of You

The funny little things that remind me of you — reflections in the surface of the river, sunlight dappling the leaves, hearing laughter wafting up from afar, the aroma of coffee... I just wanted to let you know that I'm thinking of you, it's become a very pleasant pastime.

I know you were going to hospital today and I've been thinking of you, and hoping and wishing that everything works out fine. You're not alone when you face these things you know, just as I know you would have me in your thoughts through my darker days.

Memories of you warm me like the sun on my upturned face.

When I think of you a smile comes to my face and I'm glad.

Can you feel me thinking of you? Do you suddenly feel good for no particular reason?

I was just thinking of you, and the phone rang — it was you!

My time is never wasted when I think of you!

I love to surround myself with thoughts of you — it's like living in a warm welcoming cottage.

I am thinking of you and hoping that you are happy — remember I'm only a phone call away if you need to talk about anything.

Missing You

It starts as a little niggle—something's missing—and then it comes to me. Even though I only saw you this morning when we went our separate ways, I'm missing you already. Can't wait to see you and hold you this evening. Maybe I can ring you and hear your voice.

Ever since you moved interstate, I've been missing you—I miss your friendship, the laughs we had, how we supported each other through all kinds of trials and tribulations. A true friend is hard to find, and so I just wanted you to know that I miss you. I'll ring you on the weekend.

I miss you, I miss you, I miss you!

I wonder when I'm missing you, are you missing me?

Missing you is like an ache,
and the only cure is to be with you again.

I miss your smile, your voice, your touch!

Missing someone you love—it's bittersweet!

Can't wait for you to come back from your trip—I've missed you so much!

Forgive Me Please

They say forgiveness is the best word in the English language — I can understand that—it would lighten my heart so much to know you have forgiven me.

I know I probably don't deserve this, but I need you to forgive me. I can't get past what has happened unless you do. So please let me know you have and I will make it up to you.

Please find it in your heart to forgive me. I know I've been thoughtless but I never meant to give you one moment's pain.

If you just forgive me, I'll spend every day making it up to you. I just can't go on unless you do.

Didn't mean to hurt you, can you please forgive and forget and I will learn from what I've done, promise!

I know my actions/words hurt you.
If it were possible for me to relive that moment I caused pain
the new outcome would be so different.
Please forgive me.

That was so thoughtless of me.
Can you forgive a thoughtless moment?

I am sorry.

Forgiveness Quotes

Once a woman has forgiven her man, she must not reheat his sins for breakfast. —Marlene Dietrich

It is easier to get forgiveness than permission.
—Stewart's Law of Retroaction

The weak can never forgive.
Forgiveness is the attribute of the strong. —Mahatma Gandhi

Forgiveness is a funny thing.
It warms the heart and cools the sting. —William Arthur Ward

It is easier to forgive an enemy than to forgive a friend.
—William Blake

Forgive all who have offended you, not for them, but for yourself. —Harriet Nelson

He who cannot forgive breaks the bridge over which he himself must pass. —George Herbert

Forgiveness does not change the past,
but it does enlarge the future. —Paul Boese

Never does the human soul appear so strong as when it forgoes revenge, and dares forgive an injury. —E.H. Chapin

Always forgive your enemies — nothing annoys them so much.
—Oscar Wilde

Thank You for Being My Friend

What always surprises me is
That you know all about me
And yet — you still like me!
Hell, I don't even do that!
Thank you, friend.

Someone who laughs at your jokes
Listens to your bellyaches
Encourages your dreams and schemes
But loves you even if they come to nothing.
Thank you, friend.

Someone who sticks with you no matter
Whether you're mad, glad, sad or bad!
Thank you! I'll do the same for you.

Someone who loves you better
On your worst days than you love yourself,
Who forgives you long before you stop feeling guilty
Who always puts the best spin on the things you do.
Thank you, friend!

The bird has its nest
The spiders its web
Man needs a friend
To feel at home.
Thank you, friend!

You've kept your heart
A little softer than your head
And forgiven me more times
Than you found fault
Thank you, friend!

The making of a friend
Doesn't happen in the good times
But when you're going through storms
And the others are jumping ship.
Thank you, friend, for being by my side.

You don't change when I change
Or nod when I nod
I've got a shadow for that!
I want my friend to help me, and be honest and true
Thank you, friend, thank you!

Being able to think aloud
To say a thing without worrying about offense
To have one there who puts a good spin on my motives
And always give me the benefit of the doubt.
My true friend — thank you!

Laughing when my jokes aren't that good
And sympathising when my problems aren't that bad
Thank you, friend!

You overlook my little lapses
And praise me when I've done something right.
Thank you, friend!

You are the friendly mirror
Much friendlier than the one who criticises me each morning
Thank you, friend!

Smiles, Hugs and kisses

Smiling is the curve, which sets all things straight
Smile today — go on, don't you hesitate!

If you keep smiling
It will not only hearten your friends
But your enemies will wonder
What the hell you've been up to
To make you so cheerful.

Smile especially for the one who has no more smiles to give
They are more than others in need of them.

Ever noticed how splendid your day becomes
if you live it behind a smile?
Instead of a hearty breakfast to start your day
Try smiling at yourself in the mirror
That should make a huge difference.

I remember when you gave me hugs; you wrapped your little arms
around me and squeezed with all your might.
Can I start hugging you back now?

When you don't have the words
But you just want to reach out
Go on, hug, hug, hug!

Arms wrapped around you
Warm and snug
How lovely it is!
No words needed.

Sending you a hug today
You can call upon this IOU
At any time day or night!

Darling, this is the promise of a hug.
When you think I'm mad at you,
You can demand it,
I promise I will deliver!

Now you know
We were born to hug
We love to do it
And love being on the receiving end
I promise to hug you more!

The kiss intervenes when
Words become superfluous.

Getting so close that you can't see anything wrong with the other.
That's why God invented kisses.

Coming together for a kiss
How does it ever happen?
A little miracle of trust and faith
And longing for closeness.

Get Well

Writing 'Get Well' Wishes

These are primarily for people who cannot be at the bedside of those who are unwell. If the diagnosis is not serious, keeping the tone light and humourous may be just what the doctor ordered! If this is inappropriate, another thing to mention may be something you miss about them and wish them a fast recovery.

If the illness is serious, unless you know they are particularly religious, it may be best to avoid any mention of religion, or similar, as this may offend. People who may be suffering from a serious illness may also not want the illness taken lightly or made fun of. It is best to think positive and keep it real. Not all serious illnesses are terminal so be optimistic that the recipient will soon be feeling better. With illnesses such as cancer or AIDS, there are certain side-affects, such as loss of hair, which should not be the subject of amusement, unless you are a close friend or family, and even then only done in an appropriate manner. Instead, focus on the person's character and what they have achieved in life rather than the illness itself.

Writing to sick children is different from writing to adults. If it is not terminal, it is best to let them know how brave they are being, and if you went through the same thing or something similar, it can be a good idea to tell them. Make the sick child feel missed, important and loved and always include a gift.

I'm sorry to hear you are feeling unwell. I hope you will be feeling better soon.

I was sorry to hear that you were feeling a little sick. Get well soon.

I hope this card brightens your day and brings a smile to your face.

Get well soon.
Get well wishes
From the Heart...
'Cause that's where
All good wishes start.
Have a good day,
And get lots of rest.

Best wishes for a speedy recovery.

Some people will do anything just to get breakfast in bed.
Get well soon.

Sending you my very best wishes for a speedy recovery.

Take this time to remember what is most important in life...You!
Get well soon

You are handling this illness in a very courageous manner.
You are an inspiration to us all.
Get well soon.

Illness

Friend with a sick child

Dearest friend, I know this is a very anxious time for you — please know our thoughts are with you, and I am only a phone call away if you need someone to talk to, or anything that needs to be done, whilst you're at the hospital. Know we love you, and our thoughts are with you.

Please know that you are not alone — we are thinking of you and the little one, and praying that soon he/she will be well again.

We were very saddened to hear that Jane/James was feeling unwell. We send our warmest wishes and hope that they are feeling better soon.

Friends who are ill

Dear friend, I am so sorry to hear that you're not well — please ring me if you want some company, but I will understand if you don't feel well enough. Just know you are not alone, and that I am wishing you better again.

So often they say GET WELL as if that were an order, and you could comply — just relax and recuperate and do what you have to do to let the body heal itself — our thoughts are with you.

I am so sorry to hear that you are unwell. Know that you are in my thoughts and I wish you a speedy recovery.

Friend who has just been diagnosed with terminal illness

I can hardly imagine how shocked and devastated you must be to have this news. Dear friend, just know that you have someone who will be beside you no matter what, just as you would be for me. You have been the best friend anyone could ever ask for and if I can help in any way I will.

Words can sometimes not be enough — but I offer you many, many hugs in the days ahead.

Words cannot express the sadness and deep pain I feel for you. The times ahead will be difficult and trying but know that you do not have to bear this burden alone. You will be in my thoughts and prayers and I will be there every step of the way to guide and help you through this.

May you find peace in this difficult time.

We can't choose the hand we are dealt, but we do get to decide how we play the cards. You play with courage and inspiration.

You are truly wonderful person. I am happy and proud to have you as a friend.

Bereavement

Writing Death, Grievance or Condolence Notes

When you write to a person who has lost someone close, bear in mind that this is very personal to them. When writing the note, try and comment about something memorable and special to you. Focus on how the deceased lived, not how they died. Try and avoid using age as a condolence, such as they were 'old and lived a full life.' Losing someone is the focus, not their age. Deaths within a family may bring up some complex issues such as Wills and estates or family arguments. The best course of action in this situation is if you do not have anything nice to say, say nothing at all. A condolence note is not an appropriate time to bring up past problems, or to lay blame at individuals.

Death by suicide can bring feelings of anger or guilt to people close to the deceased. In this case offer help and let the family know you are thinking of them.

At a Time of Loss

I can only imagine how hard it must be for you to be alone now – but the spirit does live on and we will hear the echoes of our beloved in the days to come.

Our thoughts and prayers are with you in this difficult time.

Death is a night
Hope is the star
And listening love
Can hear the rustling of a wing.

When you're crying look into your heart
And you'll find that you are weeping for a joy still remembered.

In dying we entrust ourselves to the hearts and minds of those we love.

Love is immortal and goes beyond the horizon of dying
We are the ones who can't see past that horizon.

Keep your loved ones alive in your mind and imagination
Talk of their life and loves often
Honour their involvement in your days.

Tears are eloquent and we should not hold them back
They speak of overwhelming sorrow, deep contrition and unspeakable love.

Just as there are seasons that each have their time and reason
So too does grief and mourning our loved ones.
Remembering will become a kinder thing once time has passed.

When someone you love dies
Wish for your peace as much as theirs
That you will be able to remember
All that is good and kind and true.

Think of the ones you have 'lost'
As not lost
Because they live on in you
You see them in your children
The smile or gesture
Give thanks that they live on.

A time for sorrow a time for tears
It seems it'll never end
As if your heart will break
But take it moment by moment
And remember what your loved one would wish for you
— to be again happy again.

Friend Who is Dying

I just needed to let you know how very special you are to me, and that I'll be here in this very difficult time – you are such an amazing person and your courage shines out like a beacon of light upon all those who meet you. All those of us lucky enough to have known you count themselves blessed.

I am going to miss you so much that I'm scared to even contemplate how empty I will feel when you are no longer here. Please know that despite feeling that I would not change a moment of the time we have had together as friends. I love you and will keep you always close to my heart.

My dearest friend, words cannot express how much your friendship has meant to me and how much I am going to miss you. Your bravery and your courage throughout these hard times is simple amazing and is one of the things I will miss about you most. You will forever be in my heart and thoughts.

Lover of Partner Who is Dying

My darling, we have lived through many things but this has to be the hardest – I can hardly imagine how I can go on without you by my side. You have been my lover, my best friend and I could have faced anything with you as my partner, but this is very, very hard, and I know it is harder even for you. Know that I am here for you and will not leave your side if you don't want me to.

I am writing this down as it is too hard to say in words. Losing you will be like losing my heart, my breath, my soul – I wish I had been better at telling you each day how much I have loved you and felt your love in return – I don't understand why I should have to live without you, but you are so courageous, and my love for you will never die.

I want you to know that you have been the love of my life – every day I have known you is a blessing – and even though I can hardly think how I will live without you, I will hold you so close to my heart and still hear your voice. Know that you are very, very special to me, and I am here to comfort you in this very difficult painful time.

I love you and that won't change no matter what happens. Love can continue beyond and I will feel your presence every day.

General Loss

I was so sorry to hear of your loss. I can only imagine how you must be feeling. I wish there was something I could do to take the pain away. Please know that I am here for you.

I just wanted you to know that I'm here for you in this time of great sorrow. We can never comprehend why this is happening. If there is anything, anything you need, know that I'm only a phone call away – but also if you need to be alone sometimes, I'll understand that as well.

The loss of a loved one is a terrible burden to bear. My thoughts are with you during this difficult time and if there is anything I can do to help, please don't hesitate to ask.

Loss of a Wife

Our hearts go out to you! Please know that we will be here for whatever you need to get you through the sadness.

I was so shocked to hear of (*name*) passing. You have my deepest condolences during this difficult time.

There are no words that can express the sadness we feel for your loss. All of us knew how very close you were – I can take the kids to school in the mornings if this will be a help and if you need other things done around the house whilst getting back on your feet please let me know. Just remember too, if you need a hug and to cry on someone's shoulder, I'll be here for you.

Loss of a Husband

My heart goes out to you in this sad, sad time. I can barely imagine what you must be feeling. I will be here for you in the tough days ahead – please let me take you out for a meal, and if you need a hand with the kids or the shopping, don't hesitate to ask. It's times like these that we need to rely on our friends to help us through – just as you would do for us.

We were so sad to hear of (*name*) passing. While things must seem really hard at the moment, please know that our thoughts are with you and our home and hearts are always open to you.

The death of (*name*) is such a tragic loss to us all. He was such a warm and caring person and the world is a sadder place now that he has gone. I know we are better people having known him and may his memory live on in all of us.

Death of Mother

I am so sorry to hear your mother has passed away. She was a wonderful person and will be missed by more than her family – I just hope you can bear the sorrow and that she will live on in you.

Your mother was such a special person and I feel for your loss. I have such fond memories of her and will miss her greatly in time to come. May her happiness and vibrancy live on through you.

(*name*) was such a delightful person and I was sad to hear that she has passed. I know she loved you very much and was so proud of you and everything you have achieved. She will be sadly missed and my thoughts are with you and your family at this time.

Death of Father

I am so sorry to hear that your father has passed away. I know you can't believe you will ever get over the sadness, but you will find as time passes that his spirit lives on in you, that we don't lose the ones who have to leave us. Our thoughts and love are with you.

My thoughts and best wishes are with you at this most difficult time. Your father was such a wonderful person and will be sadly and fondly missed. If there is anything I can do to help, please let me know.

The passing of (*name*) was such a sad and sudden loss. He was always such a wonderful father to you and loved you very much. His spirit will always live on inside of you and memories of him will never be far away. My deepest condolences.

Death of Son or Daughter

It is one of the saddest things to bear for a parent – the loss of their child – you never thought it could happen this way and my heart is breaking for you – please know that in these dark days I am here for you.

The loss of a child must be one of the most heart-breaking experiences a parent could endure. I know he/she loved you very much and you could not have been better parents to him/her. Please know that my thoughts are with you and if there is anything I can do, please let me know.

I was so sorry to hear of (*name*) passing. There is no reason why a child should die before his/her parents and while it may seem that this hurt will never go away, in time you will heal and remember all those sweet moments you shared and cherish the time you had together.

Miscarriage/Stillbirth

I know how much you anticipated the birth of your child – the thoughts and dreams involved in creating a new life. My heart goes out to you at this time – may deep peace and comfort come to you.

My thoughts are with you during this most difficult time. If you ever need to talk, please know that I am always here for you and that my heart goes out to you.

I was so sorry to hear about your loss. I know how excited you were and how much this baby meant to you, and words cannot express the sorrow I feel for you. You are both such wonderful people and I hope the future holds another special baby for you.

We want you to know how deeply we care for you and share the pain of the stillbirth of your baby. Words are so inadequate at this time but please know we will help with any practical that needs to be done, not to mention hugs at any time you need them.

Our hearts go out to you at this most difficult time. I know how much you were looking forward to the birth of your baby and the life you were going to share and build together. May you find come comfort and peace at this time and know that we are thinking of you.

Loss of Co-Worker

(*name*) was someone we all loved working with – we are going to miss him/her very much – it's very hard to find the words to console at such times but please know that we wish you peace and comfort in the days to come.

We were very sad to hear of the passing of (*name*) his/her smiling face will be missed around the office and he/she will be fondly remembered. Our thoughts are with you at this most difficult time.

Our thoughts are with you during these hard times. (*name*) was a wonderful friend and a kind and thoughtful co-worker. He/She will be greatly missed.

Death of Young Child Through an Accident

We have only just heard of little (*name*) death and can barely comprehend what you must be going through – we hold you in our hearts at this sad, sad time.

This tragic accident has shocked us and we can only imagine the pain you must feel. Our thoughts and prayers are with you and may you find the strength and courage to get you through this difficult time.

The passing of (*name*) is a terrible and tragic thing and our thoughts are with you during this time. The loss of a child must be a terrible thing to bear but your strength and your courage will see you through the dark moments.

Death of Young Child after Illness

We are so sorry for the loss of your darling child – your time together was so short and it was very sad to see a little one suffering – please know that we are here to support you and comfort you in the days ahead.

We were very saddened to hear of (*name*) passing. The courage and bravery he/she showed throughout his/her illness was extraordinary and should be an example to us all. Our thoughts and love are with you at this time and may his/her life and passing be a reminder of how precious life is.

Our deepest condolences on the passing of (*name*). While his/her life was short, I know he/she tried to live life to the fullest and touched the hearts of everyone who knew him/her. (*name*) will be remembered for his/her smile and courage in those difficult last months. Our thoughts and prayers are with you.

Death of Child through Suicide

Our thoughts are with you at this sad and confusing time when you are trying to make sense of (*name*) choice to take his/her life – as parents we do the best we can for our children and that is all we can do.

We loved (*name*) and will miss him/her very much and will always remember the good times. Please know we are here should you need a friend.

We are deeply confused and saddened by (*name*) choice to take his/her own life. I know as parent's you provided a loving and warm home for him/her and could have done nothing more. We offer our deepest condolences and heartfelt wishes that your bravery and courage will prevail in these most difficult times.

Accidental Death of a Young Adult

We can hardly imagine how devastated you must feel at the death of your darling son/daughter – as parents we do everything in our power to keep them safe from harm. So we can't comprehend when this happens. Please know you are in our thoughts and we will be there for you.

The death of a son/daughter would be one of the hardest things a parent would have to endure. The tragic passing of (*name*) so suddenly truly saddens us all and our love and thoughts are with you at this time.

This terrible, tragic accident has made us realise just how precious life is. (*name*) was a beautiful person whose love of life and his/her family and friends shone through. He/She will be sadly missed and her spirit never forgotten.

Quotes About Death and Dying

People living deeply have no fear of death.
—Anaïïs Nin, Diary, 1967

Death may be the greatest of all human blessings. —Socrates

Healthy children will not fear life if their elders have integrity enough not to fear death. —Erik H. Erikson

We understand death for the first time when he puts his hand upon one whom we love. —Madame de Stael

The death of someone we know always reminds us that we are still alive — perhaps for some purpose which we ought to re-examine. —Mignon McLaughlin, *The Neurotic's Notebook*, 1960

Relationships

Valentines Day
14th February

Hey funny little Valentine
If you agree to be all mine
I'll shout you to a glass of wine
And maybe take you out to dine.

From a secret and devout admirer
Just letting you know you are loved
From afar!

To my one and only Valentine
I love you with all my heart.

The stars have lost their luster since I looked into your eyes. The world has some meaning now that you are in my life. I love you.

Valentine's day
Is a delightful way
To make 'I love you'
So easy to say.

'Love' may mean nothing in tennis
but in life it's everything.
Come Valentine say you'll be mine

and our hearts always entwine!
I've waited with breath baited
To ask you this day
If you will be my bride
Please say 'Yes' and make me the happiest man alive!

Oh Valentine – say you'll be mine
And you'll never ever be sorry you did
For I will keep you safe from harm
And make you very happy you said 'Yes!'

Like an orchid that blooms on only one day
There's Valentine's for lovers who are too shy to say
That their heart is so full of love and caring.
Please let me know if those feelings you're sharing!

You are my hope, my help, my heart
The passion that is me,
The whole of which I am a part,
My peace, my ecstasy.

To ask you to be my Valentine's
I'd have to talk to you.
Something I'm far too shy
To have managed yet to do!

You are the gentle waves
That wash upon my shore.
Oh please, please say that you'll be mine
And I will cry no more!

With gifts and flowers they show their love
But these soon fade away.
But my love is strong and lasting
On this and every day!

Finding Love

You are the waves crashing on the shore-line of my spirit.

You're walking through the corridors of my consciousness, your footfalls are the beating of my heart.

Loving you is who I am,
its where I live,
its what I value most.

Can you read my thoughts, I often wonder?
Is this what living in someone's loving
embrace does to you?

My life is no longer counted in weeks,
months and years – it is down to the moments,
the achingly beautiful moments.

I could make inventory all day of the reasons I love you and never run out…

Love is the great mystery.
By losing yourself honestly in another,
you receive your self back as a gift.

Happiness is gazing
Into the eyes of the one you love
And finding that love lives there also.

True love cannot be found where it truly does not exist,
Nor can it be hidden where it truly does.
You are my true love and I want the whole world to know it.
I love you.

I love thee, I love but thee
With a love that shall not die
Till the sun grows cold
And the stars grow old.
—William Shakespeare

Seduce my mind and you can have my body.
Find my soul and I'm yours forever.
Win my love and you will never lose it.

Your voice makes me tremble inside
And your smile is an invitation
For my imagination to go wild.

Did my heart love till now?
Forswear it sight,
For I ne'er saw true beauty till this night.
—William Shakespeare

My love for you is a journey;
Starting at forever,
And ending at never.

You may only be one person to the world
But you are the world to me.

Love me without hesitation
Trust me without fear
Need me without demanding
Want me without limitations
Accept me without change
Desire me without inhibitions
And I will be yours forever and always.

Being deeply loved by someone gives you strength,
While loving someone deeply gives you courage.
You give me the world.

Anniversary

Writing Anniversary Notes

There are two types of anniversary notes.

1. To your spouse
2. To another couple.

When writing to a couple, it is appropriate to comment on how the marriage of these two people has made you feel or how it has set an example to you.

When writing a note to your partner, it is nice to keep the note simple yet warm and personal. For example, mention some special memories such as how you met or your first date. Recall your wedding day, show appreciation or some of the reasons you fell in love and why you still love him or her.

Spouse

To my husband – who told me I looked good in whatever dress I was wearing, and hugged me on my bad-hair days.

To my wife who has always been there for me; comfort in the darker days; sharing the moments of joy – every step of the journey has been richer for having you by my side.

For the memories of yesterday, happiness of today, promise of tomorrow. Happy Anniversary.

Being married to you makes me realise just how lucky I am.

I Love You. Happy Anniversary.

You will always be my best friend, you will always be my true love.

For always and forever...I love you. Happy Anniversary.

After all these years, a single glance or touch still makes my heart stop. I love you. Happy Anniversary.

To my darling wife/husband on our anniversary. You make my life worthwhile and I love you very much. Thank you for sharing my life with me.

To The Couple

Mum and Dad, congratulations on yet another year of togetherness – we love you very much.

Wishing you more happy years as husband and wife, may you cherish your memories and special dreams always.

To both of you. It's great to see you being such good friends to each other and finding time for your other friends as well.

Wishing you a special day that's filled with joy and happiness.

To the memories you cherish, the joys you share and the dreams you dream. Best wishes on your anniversary.

May the special joys of sharing life together be yours today and every day. Happy Anniversary.

Congratulations on your wedding anniversary. Your love and commitment to each other is an inspiration to us all.

To a very special couple on their anniversary. Congratulations and may this be the start of another great year.

May this time
be filled with new hopes
in your hearts and
new dreams in your minds.

To a special couple who have travelled through life hand in hand. Happy Anniversary.

Mothers And Fathers

Mothers Day

Mummy, Mummy you've been so swell
To carry me for nine months and raise me as well
I want to take you out to dinner
And celebrate my Mum, the winner!

How can I thank you enough, my dearest Mum
For everything you've done?
How can I thank you, my dearest Mum
You are the dearest one!

My Mum, the one and only – how can I ever thank you enough for being there for me right from the start!

We love you! We appreciate you for all you are and all you do.

To our Mother, the most beloved woman in our lives.

My Mum! When we were young and there wasn't enough to go round
You suddenly didn't feel like pie any more
And that's the way you've raised us, putting us first each time
Now we're here to thank you, and put you first.

M is for the many things she gave me,
O means there is no other,
T is for the tears she cried sometimes,
H is for her generous heart;
E is for her eyes which shine with love,
R is for reflection on what it means to be,
Put them all together, they spell MOTHER,
A word that means the world to me.

She carries you under her heart
She dandles you on her knee
She ties up your shoes she fixes your hurts
She makes you feel loved, she makes you feel good
– thank you Mum, you're the best that can be!

You loved me before I was born
You made it a leap of faith
You answered my cries
You healed all my hurts
Dearest Mum bless you!

When I was born you held me close
You smiled and fell in love
You fed me, kissed me, hugged me
Taught me how to speak
And when I was quite naughty you turned the other cheek;
Mum—Thank you for being so loving!

When I went round the Merry Go Round
I waved each time and you waved back
You've been there for me all my life
Thank you dearest Mum!

None of us asked to be born, it's true
But I'm so happy that God picked you
To be my Mum!

You taught me to walk,
You taught me to talk
You taught me to tie my shoes
You mopped up my tears
You banished my fears
Thank you Mum! Happy Day

When first your ears-in-progress
took in the comforting beat
of your Mother's heart...

Thank you Mum
For growing me so close
For holding me in your loving embrace!

I could search the whole world over
for a thousand years and more
and never find a better Mum than you.

Just a simple thank you
Is all that I can say
To my very special Mum
On her very special day.

Fathers Day

A father is special, a father is kind
He's cared for us night and day
He's given us love with his heart and mind
And been there to laugh and play.

Fathers hold their children's hands
for just a little while
But their hearts forever.

Dad we love you! We don't thank you often enough for all the care and love you show us.

To my Dad! I've been so lucky to have you in my life – you have taken care of me ever since I was a baby and continue to be there for me every single day. Thank you!

F is for the fondness you've always shown to me
A is for attention to the smallest little things
T is for the tenderness when I was sad you see
H is for his happy smile, such joy it always brings
E is for his easy and understanding ways
R is for reflections of a man who so loved me
Happy Fathers Day, dear Dad! On that we'll both agree.

Thank you Dad for listening and caring. For giving and sharing, But especially for just being you! Happy Fathers Day

Guide, friend, teacher, role-model – My Dad!
Happy Fathers Day! I love you.

I opened my eyes for the very first time
You were there
I fell and hurt my knee
You were there
I needed a lift from the dance
You were there
Thank you DAD! You've been so good to me.

From the very first step
To every step of the way
You've always been there for me
Thank you Dad!

Dad, I don't tell you nearly often enough
But you're always in my thoughts and I love you very much.
Happy Fathers Day!

You lifted me up and never let me down
You set limits but still you let me fly
I'm so glad you're my Dad!

Dad you are the kind of father
Who makes me want to be the best father I can be
Happy Fathers Day!

My Dad, he knows me so well,
since before I was born
and loves me anyway!
Happy Fathers Day!

Life can be hard to figure sometimes
And I can't find the solution on my own
I go to my Dad, he listens then comes up with gentle suggestions
and suddenly it's clear.
Thank you Dad! Happy Father's Day!

Today is your special day
Relax and have fun in it.

Thank you Dad, for caring and being there.

Bon Voyage

Don't be dismayed at good-byes. A farewell is necessary before you can meet again. And meeting again after a moment or lifetime is certain for those who are friends. — Richard Bach

Bon Voyage

It's so hard to say goodbye, especially when we don't know how long before we meet again. But whether it's a month or years, it won't change my love for you. Please stay in touch.

Bon Voyage and the very best on your travels!
Such a pity we can't go with you, but our thoughts will.
Remember us waiting here on the shores and wishing you well.

Have a wonderful holiday! Drink in all the new sensations, and even if things don't go exactly as planned, think of the wonderful travel stories you'll be able to tell us.

Not all those who wander are lost.

Have a fantastic trip and I look forward to seeing all the photos when you return!

Have a safe trip and while I cannot be with you, my thoughts will be. Make sure to take lots of photos and have lots of fun!

Achievements

Success: To laugh often and much, to win the respect of intelligent people and the affection of children, to earn the appreciation of honest critics and endure the betrayal of false friends, to appreciate beauty, to find the best in others, to leave the world a bit better, whether by a healthy child, a garden patch, or a redeemed social condition; to know even one life has breathed easier because you have lived. This is to have succeeded!

—Ralph Waldo Emerson

Encouragement

If at first you do succeed, hip hip hooray! If it takes you a few tries to get it right, who's counting?

Do what you love and have a passion for and the rest will follow! Good luck in everything you do.

The way to succeed at anything is to hang on for that bit longer when all the others have given up. Good luck with your new venture!

Do what you love the most and you will never fail – that comes before anything.

Unquenchable enthusiasm and dogged persistence are the ingredients for success in any field – just ask the entrepreneurs. Good luck!

Make sure that you work at your happiness levels – it helps you want what you get when you get it! Good luck in your enterprise.

Special Awards or Honours

Congratulations! You deserve this award. You have worked so hard and remained so committed to putting in the effort. May this just be the start of many, many milestones of achievement.

Well done in receiving this special award. Your long hours of training and hard work have finally paid off. Congratulations.

What a fantastic result! You have worked and trained so hard, it is great to see all of that hard work recognised. Congratulations!

Congratulations on being chosen to represent the school in debating/quiz night/battle of the minds/rock eisteddford. We will wait to hear how you went and remember that even getting to this point is such an accomplishment. Good on you!

Well done on receiving this most special award. All of your hard work and patience has finally paid off and we are very proud of you. May this be the first of many more to come.

My most sincere congratulations. You did it!
Where others may have faltered you pressed on
to the successful end. Well done!

Graduation

Congratulations! This is a wonderful achievement and just the beginning of your career and the fulfilment of your aspirations – we wish you every good fortune.

Congratulations!
How well you've done to get through your exams, and stick with the years of hard work – here's hoping that whatever you have planned will come to pass.

Congratulations on your graduation. Your years of hard work have finally paid off and now you have the knowledge and the experience behind you to move into the next exciting part of your life.

You are finally ready to leap into the world head first and start achieving some of your dreams! Well Done and Good Luck!

Launch of Entrepreneurial Venture

Bravo! We wish you every success in this venture – you have worked very hard to get to this point and it takes a lot of courage to launch into something on your own. But you are so talented that we have no doubt this will be just the beginning of wonderful things for you.

Congratulations the starting of this new adventure. With your determination and talent, we have every reason to believe that this will be the very success you imagined it would be. Your courage is an example to us all.

May your cash flow be plentiful, you overheads low and your customers satisfied!

Starting a new business involves a lot of hard work but I know that you are prepared to go all the way and make a success of this. I wish you the best of luck and if there is anything I can do to help, please let me know.

Success/Failure Quotes

Don't aim for success if you want it; just do what you love and believe in, and it will come naturally. —David Frost

Some people dream of success...while others wake up and work hard at it.

Judge your success by what you had to give up in order to get it. The two hardest things to handle in life are failure and success. Pray that success will not come any faster than you are able to endure it. —Elbert Hubbard

There is only one success — to be able to spend your life in your own way. —Christopher Morley

Flaming enthusiasm, backed up by horse-sense and persistence, is the quality that most frequently makes for success.
—Dale Carnegie

Success is getting what you want; happiness is wanting what you get.

Success is how high you bounce when you hit bottom.
—George Smith Patton

Accommodation

Home, the spot of earth supremely blest,
A dearer, sweeter spot than all the rest.
—Robert Montgomery

Teen Moving Out First Time

A big step for you, a small step for mankind.

May your friends bring you food and drink, and not mess the carpet.

May your landlord understanding when you're a day or two late on the rent.

May these walls be a happy home to you.

Don't turn the music up too loud, remember to take out the garbage, and that your mum isn't around to pick up after you. And if you want to eat, you have to buy the food.

Moving House

New neighbourhood, hearth and house, blessings to all who live within – may you, hear the patter of little children, the scurrying of pets, the aroma of good food, and the laughter of good friends gathered.

Congratulations on the purchase of your new house! Moving house is always very exciting and a lot of hard work but it will all be worth it. We look forward to seeing your new home once you have settled in.

Goodbye and good luck! Parting is difficult but life is full of change and moving is just one of life's realities – I hope you find happiness in your new house and city, and that you won't forget your good friends left behind.

We are sorry to see you leave but we are thrilled for you on the purchase of your new house. Congratulations and best of luck!

Housewarming

God bless this house! May the roof stay strong and the plumbing too. May the walls protect you from storms. May you sigh with pleasure each time you come home! May the housework be less than the times you relax and enjoy!

Good fortune to you in this new abode – may the walls ring with laughter, and the halls be redolent with the aroma of food and flowers!

To your new home
Which isn't just an address
It's where they understand you
And welcome you back each time!

Bless your new home
Peace from the troubles of the world
Hugs when you need them
People in your corner when things get tough!

Bless this home and the new beginning
May your family have many happy times
And enjoy warmth and shelter and love.

A Successful Auction

We've just heard that the auction on Saturday was a big success and that you made your reserve price – congratulations, this is cause for celebration! You have both worked so hard leading up to this point and it's just great when plans work out.

Congratulations on a successful action. You must be very pleased with the outcome and reaching your reserve price. We look forward to visiting you in your new home once you have settled in.

Quotes On 'Home'

Home is not where you live but where they understand you.
—Christian Morgenstern

Home is a place not only of strong affections, but of entire unreserve; it is life's undress rehearsal, its backroom, its dressing room. —Harriet Beecher Stowe

Peace — that was the other name for home. —Kathleen Norris

Home is a place you grow up wanting to leave, and grow old
wanting to get back to. —John Ed Pearce

A house is a home to call your own.
Walls that hear your laughter, floors that catch you tears
every room a secret hiding place to turn away your fears.
In your house you will never be alone
when you make it your home.

Any builder can build you a house,
but only you can make it a home.
—T.P. Carolat

Home is where the heart is.

Wherever I may wonder,
There's no place like home.

Nothing is more welcome than
the sound of your own front door.

Home is home, be it never so homely.
—Hesba Stretton

Working Life

First Job

Congratulations on getting your very first job – we know you can make a success of this, and that you'll go from strength to strength – things will seem strange at the start but you won't take long fitting right in.

Well done on getting your first job! The work force is not an easy place to break into and you have done exceptionally well on getting in there. Congratulations.

On Taking a 'Seachange'

We are so happy you've made this decision to stop and smell the roses a little more often – we are sure your new life is going to be full of so many good things and you will wake every morning and feel great to be alive. Congratulations and all the best.

The wise man is one who gives up on work,
before it gives up on him.

So you're giving up workaholism and all its charms – how will you manage to fill your leisure hours?

The funny thing about earning more money is that you still manage to spend it all.

Getting Promoted

Congratulations – you deserve this! The best of luck to you in this new challenge – let us know how you are getting on.

Congratulations – you're climbing the ladder – remember to take care of the ones on the steps below you, just in case you meet them coming down again.

Congratulations – all the time and effort you put in has finally paid off! Job well done.

Congratulations! We never doubted you would get to the top of your profession – we have followed your illustrious rise with baited breath – you deserve this job, and we wish you every good fortune in this your latest challenge.

Congratulations, I hope you get everything you deserve.

Well-Liked Colleague Leaving Job

We're going to miss your vivacity, audacity and tenacity.

It's been such a pleasure working with you, –good fortune!

The office just won't be the same – keep in touch!

You've brightened our lives and lightened our work load!

Retiring

Dearest friend, it's been such a pleasure working alongside you these years, and we are going to miss you very much here at the office – hope I can call you informally sometimes if we need your expertise. I hope your new life will be everything you hoped for. Hope we can stay in touch no matter what – of course we're all envious!

Remember when you have nothing to do, do it well!

Why is it that when a man retires to a life where time should no longer matter, he is presented with a watch?

When a man retires, his wife gets twice the husband but only half the income. —Chi Chi Rodriguez

Here's to a job well done.

Retirement. So many possibilities.

Now you can wake up and say.
'Good morning, God!' rather than
'Good God, it's morning!'

Invitations

Invitations can be as creative or as unusual as you like, however there are certain things to remember when sending invitations.

Checklist:

1. Time
2. Date
3. Place
4. RSVP date
5. RSVP contact details
6. Dress code (*if required*)
7. Map (*if required*)

If you do not wish to receive gifts on this occasion, it is appropriate to state this on the invitation. If you are sending invitations to out-of-town guests, make sure the invitations are sent out at least 3 to 4 weeks in advance to allow guest plenty of time to arrange transport and accommodation. Other invitations can be sent out with 2 to 3 weeks notice.

Birthday Party

Children's Birthday

Share the fun
at Margot's
3rd birthday!
Sunday, November 30
4:00 PM
72 The Avenue
SOMEPLACE

R.S.V.P. 1234 5678

Please Join Us
In Celebration of
Margot's 3rd Birthday
Sunday, November 30
4:00 p.m. — 6:00 p.m.

Margot's House
72 The Avenue
SOMEPLACE

General Birthday

Please come and help me celebrate my 31st Birthday
Please join me for dinner on Friday January 13th, 2005 at
(*place and address*)
RSVP January 7
Ph 1234 5678

Milestone Birthday

In Case You Didn't Know…
David is turning the BIG 5-0!
Come and help us celebrate this momentous occasion
with a birthday BBQ!
Saturday April 5, 2005 at 7.00pm
(*address*)
RSVP March 27
Ph 1234 5678

Please join us for a birthday dinner
in honour of
Belinda's 40th Birthday.
Saturday, October 23rd at 7.00 p.m.
(*place*)
(*address*)

Surprise Party

Shhh!
It's a Surprise Birthday Party
Honouring
Anna Carter

Saturday, September 16 at 7.00 p.m.
(*place*)
(*address*)

Hosted By..

RSVP only 1234 5678

Engagement

We would love it if
you join us for a party
to announce our engagement
on May 25th
(*place*)
(*address*)
Michelle and Paul

Introducing the future
Mr. and Mrs. ....

Please join us for an
engagement party
honouring
Michelle and Paul
on May 25, 2006
at 6:00 pm
(*place*)
(*address*)
Mr. and Mrs. Canton

Bridal Showers

Katherine, Laura and Tiffany
invite you to attend the
Bridal Shower
in honour of

....

on Sunday, August 12
at 3.00 p.m.
(*place*)
(*address*)

It's all hearts and flowers!
Bridal Shower
Honouring ....
on February 21
at 4:00 pm
(*place*)
(*address*)

Wedding

The examples given are intended only as a guide. They can of course be changed to suit the style of the wedding; to read more formally or more casually. Adding a short phrase or lines from a poem to the beginning of your invitation is a great way to help create something more unusual and unique.

Host Line

A traditional format has the bride's parents hosting and inviting the guests.

Mr. and Mrs. ....

If the groom's parents are sharing the expenses, both sets of parents act as hosts, with the bride's listed first.

Mr. and Mrs. ....and Mr. and Mrs. ....

Many couples wish to mention the groom's parents, even if they're not co-hosting the wedding.

Mr. and Mrs. ....
request the honour of your presence
at the marriage of their daughter
....
to
....
Son of Mr. and Mrs. ....

Divorced parents should be listed on separate lines, with the mother's name first.

When either, or both, of the bride's parents has remarried, it's most proper that only the natural parents are listed, since they usually give the bride away; depending on your family's situation, though, step-parents can be included.

A good way not leave anyone out is to invite the guests yourselves, and mention both families.

Together with their families
(*Bride's name*) and (*Groom's name*)

More couples are paying for their own weddings and playing hosts by themselves.

(*Bride's name*)
And
(*Groom's name)*

Request Lines

By strict convention, 'the honour of your presence' is reserved for religious ceremonies.

Request the honour of your presence at the marriage of their daughter

For weddings held at a hotel or a home, it's more appropriate to use warmer, less formal wording.

Request the pleasure of your company at the marriage of their daughter.

Many families are opting to mix tradition with their own sentiments.

Would be honoured to have you share in the joy
of the marriage of their children

Couples may also issue a simple request, emphasising the celebration.

Invite you to celebrate their marriage

Date and Time Lines

Spelling out the day, date, and year lends sophistication, but you can also use a numeral for the year. Similarly, although 'half after six o'clock' is classic, it may not be right for a less formal wedding. When stating the time, only the hour is necessary; there's no need to note A.M. or P.M.

Where time of day may be unclear use 'in the morning' or 'in the evening'.

Location line

Make sure you have the proper name of your church. As with everything else, spell out 'Saint' or any other abbreviations (except R.S.V.P.). Direction cards have become a common way to direct your guests to both the ceremony and reception site. Invitations are typically written without punctuation; line breaks take the place of commas, except to separate city and state, or to avoid confusion.

(*Bride's parent's names*)
joyously invite you
to the wedding celebration of
(*Bride's name*)
and
(*Groom's name*)
Saturday the twentieth of June
(*date*)
(*place*)
(*address*)

(*Bride and Groom's names*)
invite you
to witness their wedding
and celebrate
the beginning of
their lives together
on (*date*)
at 3:30 in the afternoon
(*place*)
(*address*)

Join us for a day in the country
and share in our happiness
as we celebrate our marriage
with family and friends.
Saturday (*date*)
Half past two in the afternoon
(*place*)
(*address*)
reception immediately following
The wedding of (*Bride's name*) and (*Groom's name*)

Baby Shower

(*Name of Mother*) is having a baby!
Let's get her prepared for his/her arrival
We'll shower her with gifts for the precious little one,
We hope to see you there
Sunday April 24
three-thirty
(*place*)
RSVP to (*name and phone number*)

A baby shower
in honour of
(*Name of Mother*)
Sunday November twenty-fourth
at 4.30pm
(*place*)
(*address*)

Given by (*Hostess' name*)

Christening/Baptism

You are invited to join us
as our daughter is christened/baptised
on Sunday, (*date*)
at eleven o'clock in the morning.
(*place*)
(*address*)

Bar Mitzvah

With great pride and joy
we invite you to share a special moment in our lives
when our son, (Son's name)
will be called to the Torah as a Bar Mitzvah
on Saturday, (*date*)
at eleven o'clock in the morning
(*place*)
(*address*)

(*Parent's Names*)